THE PASSION OF THE RABBIT GOD

Hongwei Bao grew up in Inner Mongolia, China, and lives in Nottingham, UK. He teaches at the University of Nottingham. As a bilingual writer, he uses poetry, short story and creative nonfiction to explore queer desire, Asian identity, diasporic positionality and transcultural intimacy.

His creative work has appeared in *Cha: An Asian Literary Journal*, *Ink, Sweat & Tears*, *Messy Misfits Club*, *Migrant Diaries*, *Shanghai Literary Review*, *The Hooghly Review*, *The Ponder Review*, *The Rialto*, *the other side of hope*, *The Voice & Verse Poetry Magazine* and *Write On*. His work has also been featured in anthologies such as *Allegheny Nonfiction Anthology*, *Maria Lazar: Poetry from Exile*, *Queer Reparative Poetry Anthology* and *The Plaza Prizes Anthology One*. His flash fiction 'A Postcard from Berlin' won the second prize for the Plaza Prize for Microfiction in 2023.

He can sometimes be found in Nottingham's pubs performing poetry and enjoying a beer.

The Passion of the Rabbit God
兔兒神之生死愛慾

poems by
Hongwei Bao
包宏偉

Valley Press

First published in 2024 by Valley Press
Woodend, The Crescent, Scarborough, UK, YO11 2PW
www.valleypressuk.com

ISBN 978-1-915606-38-9
Cat. no. VP0226

Copyright © Hongwei Bao 2024

The right of Hongwei Bao to be identified as the author of this work has been asserted in accordance with the Copyright, Designs and Patents Act 1988.

All rights reserved. No part of this publication may be reproduced, stored in or introduced into a retrieval system, or transmitted in any form, by any means (electronic, mechanical, photocopying, recording or otherwise) without prior written permission from the rights holders.

Cover and text design by Jamie McGarry.

Contents

Passion 9

I. OLD TALES RETOLD

Confession of the Rabbit God 10
The Passion of the Rabbit God 13
Qu Yuan 15
Butterfly Lovers 17
Chang'e 19

II. NOTES ON BELONGING

But Where Do You Really Come From? 21
Why I Write in English 22
At the Opticians 25
Magic Pot 27
Leather Jacket 28
Wildest Dreams 30
Pond 32
Curve 33
Hero 34
Suitcase 38
Diaspora 40

III. QUEER INTIMACIES

Misunderstanding 41
On a Northern Train 43
Waltzing on the Pavement 44
In the Printer Room 45
In Front of the Left Lion 46
Leather Man 49
Skin 50
Ring 51

Morning Tea 52
Calling Home 53
The World's End 55
Fireflies 59
The Key 60

IV. STORIES OF OUTRAGE AND HOPE

Haunted Village 61
April in Shanghai 62
White Paper 63
Liverpool, 1946 64
Oriental Pavilion 66
A Trip to the Peak District 69
Eurovision 70
Eurostar 72
Christmas in Beeston 73
Lunar New Year 74
Snow in March 76

Acknowledgments 81

This book is dedicated to the Rabbit God (兔兒神)
a.k.a. Hu Tianbao (胡天保)
the patron god of LGBTQ+ people in Asia.

*May your glory and benevolence
forever accompany and bless
all the queers, Asians and queer Asians
whose love, imagination and creativity
know no boundary.*

Passion

Why
is passion, a strong
emotion and deep
sentimental attachment,
also an experience
of extreme suffering
and painful death?

And why
is it the name
given to a fruit?
So sweet,
so delicious,
and yet so intoxicating
that I forget
the bitterness
that comes with it.

Confession of the Rabbit God

According to the Qing Dynasty Chinese scholar Yuan Mei's short story collection What the Master Would Not Discuss (子不語, 1788), *a clerk named Hu Tianbao (胡天保) from South China's Fujian Province was found following a government official around and even peeking at the official's nude body. Hu was arrested and put on trial. Yuan didn't give much detail about the trial in his writing. This is what I imagine Hu's speech could have looked like.*

My honourable sir,
please forgive
me for following
you like a shadow.
Excuse my boldness
to desire your body.
I've upset you. My offence
has no excuse. I'm here
to give my own defence.

There's a sensation
in this world called
se (色 beauty),
It's possessed by women
as well as by men.
There's a feeling
amongst all beings named
yu (慾 desire).
Even Confucius the Sage couldn't
deny it. Nor could he expect
anyone to repress it.

Emperor Ai of Han Dynasty cut
the long sleeve of his robe,
so his beloved Dong Xian could
have a late morning sleep-in.
Lord Ling of Wei shared
a peach with his favourite Mi Zixia.

Their happy smiles outshone
the bright flowers in the orchard.
My feeling for you is no
different.

Our southern province of Fujian
is well-known for *nanfeng*.
Whether this refers to 南風 (southern style)
or 男風 (male style)
is for the wise to decide.
Men live with men, swearing
fraternity and lifelong commitment.
Women live with women, brushing
hair for each other till death.
Generation after generation
they prosper and perish.

I fell for you, my dearest
sir, the first time I saw
you. I look up to your stature,
as grand as the Mount Tai.
I admire your composure,
as calm as a pine tree.
I marvel at your knowledge
and wisdom, as deep
as the East Sea. I desire
your beauty, as delicate
as cherry blossoms.

I dream
of you each night,
and take delight
in seeing you every morning.
How I long
to stay close, smelling
your scent, touching
your skin.

My heart's desire
can't be fulfilled.
A tormented soul
only I know I have.
I'm humble,
but my love is not.
If Emperor Wei and Lord Ling
were here today, they'd give me
their blessings.

My kindest sir, I readily
leave myself at your mercy,
anticipating the harshest
punishment. But I beg
your forgiveness, my most
generous sir. My love
for you is for all to see.
Heaven and earth
bear my witness.

Hu Tianbao was sentenced to death immediately after this speech. In the underworld, the God of the Dead was touched by his story and appointed Hu as the Rabbit God (兔兒神), the patron god of queer people. Today, temples specifically dedicated to the Rabbit God can still be found in many parts of East and Southeast Asia.

The Passion of the Rabbit God

They call me the Rabbit
God because rabbit is slang
for men who love men,
women who love women,
and people whose love is not
recognised by society.

I was condemned
to death by the very man
I loved, the man whose beauty
I admired, whose shadow
I followed, whose body
I desired. He didn't appreciate
my love. He doesn't deserve
my memory.

And yet I was interrogated,
forced to confess my desire,
taunted for my audacity
and sincerity for who
I am, by whom
I love.

Crossing
a hundred mountains
and a thousand rivers,
I stood before Yanluowang,
God of the Dead and King
of the Underworld. He didn't
laugh at me. (He knew better.)

*Too many fools
in the human world*, he said,
*ignorant about love
and not deserving
to be loved. From now on
you shall be the Rabbit God,*

*the patron saint of all
your people. You shall be
their protector and guardian.
You shall bear witness
to their love. May your people
live and prosper
generation after generation.*

(Who'd have thought
the Underworld has more
wisdom and justice?)

Sitting on the altar, I see
in this mortal world
queer people driven
out of their homes,
their lands, their homelands,
queer people with no place
to call home, no right
to justice.

Come to my temple,
my dear children, I shall
offer you sanctuary,
bless you with my magic,
and witness your love
as it buds, blossoms and spreads.
Like flowers.
Like grass.
Like fire.

Qu Yuan

Qu Yuan (屈原 c. 339 – c. 278 BCE) was a classical Chinese poet who committed suicide by jumping into a river. The annual Dragon Boat Festival, or Duanwu Festival, is celebrated after him.

As I threw myself into the Miluo River, I felt the glare
of the sun, the whisper of the wind, the splash of the cold

water breaking into a thousand tiny waves, rippling,
reverberating, glistening in the bright sunlight. I plunged

deep into the sandy riverbed, where my lips were kissed
by the fish, feet tickled by the weeds, which all reminded

me of you, my dear king, your smile, your kiss, my
pounding heart, your peach-coloured cheeks. Our time

was short, because of your weakness, and the rumours
spread in the royal court by petty bystanders, those who

disliked me, who envied us. What intrigues! What malicious
lies! They say I sacrificed myself for the nation. I didn't.

The kingdom means nothing to me. All its pompousness,
pretentiousness, emptiness. But you, my love, you are my

Muse. You are the only reason for all my verses. Please don't
let them fall into the hands of those people. They don't deserve

to read my poems. They won't appreciate my affection
for you, and our feelings for each other. Remember me,

every year on the fifth day of the fifth month, when the crescent
moon climbs up the sky, when its silver light is cast on the river,

when the water is calm and clean. Think of the many
happy days we've had together. Please don't shed tears.

Take delight eating rice dumplings in my memory, unwrapping
the green bamboo leaves, feeling the warmth of my tongue, the taste

of me in your mouth. Please don't throw dumplings into the river
while the poor are starving, or allow dragon boats to roar

on the canal, in my name, for the thunderous noise will disturb
the quiet life of the fish, the plants, my spirit, the river ghosts.

Butterfly Lovers

Butterfly Lovers, also known as Liangzhu (梁祝, or Liang Shanbo and Zhu Yingtai 梁山伯與祝英臺), is a classical Chinese folk tale about the love between a man (Liang Shanbo) and a woman (Zhu Yingtai) who cross-dressed as a man.

Shanbo, can't you see
the person who's accompanied
you for three years
in the classroom,
the study, and our shared
dormitory, is not a man?

Nor am I the woman
I was before I came
in a man's disguise
to the school where women
weren't allowed.
I refused to have my fate
sealed by the red ribbons
of an arranged marriage
with a stranger I'd never
met before.

I am your Yingtai,
the person who loves you
dearly, whom you care about
deeply, with whom you shared
many sleepless nights together,
when our silhouettes
were printed on the windows,
illuminated by flickering candle lights.
Like my passion, dancing.
Like your desire, flowing.

Don't ask
if I'm a man or a woman.
Don't attempt

to give our love a name,
a name the others won't
understand, a name this
secular world doesn't deserve.

Can't you see I am
a butterfly,
my body, my mind, my spirit,
metamorphosing?
Can't you see we are
becoming a pair
of butterflies,
as I throw myself
to your tombstone,
and as we both rise
from the earth?

Together,
we'll be chasing
the flowers, the dewdrops,
the blue sky, the morning sun.

Chang'e

Chang'e (嫦娥) is known as the moon goddess in Chinese mythology.

On full-moon nights, if you look up to the sky, you'll see
me cross the lunar sea, wandering in the fragrance of osmanthus,
accompanied by my beloved jade white bunny. Stop

pitying me for my loneliness or misery, for I have
none of them. Men have composed numerous verses
to praise me, pens flowing with lust for my beauty. They

have invented countless lies to defame, to warn of me –
jealous of what they can't have. What no one can.
They say I'm greedy, selfish, and vain, a femme

fatale. They say I betrayed my husband, Hou Yi,
an 'honourable man'. Lies. These are all his lies.
My husband hasn't mentioned the beatings, his affairs,

my tears on those long, sleepless nights. Don't be fooled
by him. By society, by his kind. The day I lost my courage
to live, I swallowed all the pills in the fridge,

unaware they were not for sleep, but longevity;
my husband had kept them for himself, so his tyranny
would last forever. (How ridiculous!) In trance, my body

became lighter and lighter, like a feather, like a cloud,
rising to the air, descending on the moon. Here I met
my sisters, who shared similar experiences. We care

for one another. We plant osmanthus and raise
bunnies. Who says the moon is a cold, lonely and desolate
place? I couldn't be happier here. I don't miss the earth,

that dirty, polluted planet where lies and violence
abound, from which arrogant men send spaceships
to planets – one after another – some bearing my name,

claiming 'science', but truly, seeking a beauty they can
only dream of, born from a lie repeated a thousand times
of the 'femme fatale' banished to, imprisoned on, the moon.

But Where Do You Really Come From?

after the Fulani/Hussey conversation, 1 December 2022

I come from a remote land
one that can't be found on the map
one where there's no country or nation
    no custom or border control
    no native or foreigner
    no migrant or refugee
    no male or female
    no cis or trans
    no straight or gay
one where everyone feels at home
    in their body and skin
    in each other's company
one where no one feels the need
    to ask or answer
    where are you from
    but where do you really come from

Why I Write in English

Why do I write
in English,
a language I wasn't
born into? A language
that took me years
to learn? A language
in which I can never
expect to become
fully fluent, native?

My school imposed
English on me
when China opened its doors
to the world after decades
of Cold War isolation.
The teacher – who used to teach
Russian – taught
herself English so she could
teach us.
How are you? She'd ask.
I'm fine, thank you, and you? We'd chant.
I'm fine, thank you. She'd reply.
Even a teacher
as knowledgeable as she was
couldn't explain why anyone
would say such meaningless
things, or why we should
never say *I'm not fine*.

My university imposed
English on me when
English was a prerequisite
for exams and job interviews,
and when the dream
of studying abroad captured
every student's imagination.

At the lectern
the teacher was talking about
Marx, Mao, Deng ...
In my seat I was repeating
abasement, abbreviation, abdication ...
At night I laid the English
dictionary under my pillow.
My dreams were overflowing
with correct tenses.

I finally got a chance
to study abroad.
I had to unlearn and relearn
everything. *Write
properly*, the professor
warned, *pay attention
to your grammar!*
Speak slowly, the landlady
cautioned, *don't
swallow sounds!*

In shame and tears,
I observed the pages turning
red with each and every
tracked change. My tongue
was tied. I struggled
to make sounds.

Then *he* walked
into my life, with a sunny
smile. He didn't
notice my mistakes.
He laughed
at my jokes.
I found myself talking
at ease in front of him,
and relaxed in his arms.

Those
were my happiest days,
when the sun always shone
and the sky was aways blue.
Gradually
English had become
my best friend,
my life, my whole world.
I gave up
my mother tongue and let English
wrap up
    my body,
        my mind,
            my unconscious.

Now I write
in English,
in plain English,
in broken English,
in hybrid English.
The English language –
arrogant and proud,
with a violent past –
has adopted
me. It offers me
a shelter, while
I use my pen and voice
to subvert it
from within.

At the Opticians

That bright, orange
hot air balloon,
as if caught on fire,
permanently hangs
in the air between
the blue sky
and the green grass.
A narrowing road cuts
across the field.

A burst of air
explodes. I blink.
My eyelashes
shiver in shock.

A glare of bright,
white light burns
my vision, swallows
my consciousness.
The world disappears.
I vanish. A moment
of silence lasts
a hundred years.

The world is back
in its full lucidity.
The letters, thin and fat,
line up on the white
screen, jumping
around through constantly
shifting lenses, begging
for my recognition.

You ask me if *this* is clearer
or *that* is clearer until I start
to doubt my own judgment.
Am I sure about this?

In real life these differences
don't matter. They really
don't.

You ask me
about my medical history
family history, career history,
trying to understand
the reasons behind
my visual impairment.

Yes, Doctor –
years of hard work
have taken their toll
on my eyesight.
My love for books
has not helped.

I've never known
what a perfect world
looks like, and never
will. But that's OK,
as long as I can still
read and write
about the things
I love and care about
in my small
and imperfect world
of restricted vision.

Magic Pot

A man
from a remote land
brought in a magic
pot. Fire
blazed. Pot
turned. Sweet
aroma filled
the air.

A loud
explosion broke
the silence of spring,
waking up
the sleeping birds.
Heaven thundered.
Earth shattered.
Children screamed
in euphoria.

Gently
he smiled. His eye
wrinkles spread
wide as the white
popcorn flowed
into the children's
hands and mouths.

At sunset,
the whole village
was beaming
with creamy smiles.
Quietly
the man tucked
away his magic pot,
walking
out of the village,
into the children's
dreams.

Leather Jacket

Every time
I walked past, I couldn't help
looking at the brown
leather jacket hanging
in the shop window,
smiling

at me.
I could imagine how nice
it would look on my body,
like the one you had
on yours

that made my heart
jump.

I saved up
and bought the jacket.
It felt smooth
and supple, hugging
me gently,
like the touch
of you
(if I could touch you).

The next day
I wore it to school.
My eyes were searching
for you, like a boat
searching for a lighthouse
on a stormy night.

In the corridor
we met,
I said *hi*,
you said *hi*
and then we
parted.

Perhaps you didn't
notice my new jacket.

Wildest Dreams

I used to lie
on the floor with you
talking about our
wildest dreams.

We couldn't
wait to grow up,
to explore an unknown
adult world and all
our future adventures.

The room was quiet,
The air was heavy.
The cicadas were loud.

My hand shi-ver-ed
    as it moved
        towards you.

My hand was heavy.
My throat was dry.
My lips were tight.

We lay still
in silence.

As the pendulum clock
ticked, second
by second,

we listened
to each other's
heart, beat
by beat.

And we grew
up.

Years later,
I congratulated you
and your wife
on your marriage.

There was a brief silence
on the other side
of the line

which reminded me
of that midsummer
afternoon when we
lay on the floor talking
about our wildest
dreams.

Pond

A pond
      hidden behind lush trees
      shielded by tall reeds
      surrounded by golden daffodils.
Flying birds
      had their shadows printed
      on the mirroring water surface.
Swimming ducks
      bumped into waterlilies, dispersing
      them here and there.
A breeze
      revealed thousands of wrinkles,
      like golden fish scales
      glittering in the sun.

I visited the pond
      when I thought
      of you
      and the afternoons
      we spent together,
      feeling
      the warm sun,
      the gentle breeze,
      your hands,
      my heartbeats.

Curve

In memory of queer artist Ren Hang (1987-2017)

Is the curve you drew
    with your own body, descending
        from a high-rise, pulled
      down by gravity, breaking
    the chilly spring wind
a line of beauty?

Has it ceased screaming
    at you?
Has the endless chase
    stopped?
Are all nightmares
    over?

I want to tell you
    your smile,
        your body,
            your heart,
                have the most beautiful curves
              I have ever seen
           in this dusty,
        secular,
    suffocating
city.

Hero

    I held you tight on the back of the motorbike.
The cutting wind bit my cheeks, but I felt safe, and warm.

    You were my hero,
as I went with you to endless dates, parties, gigs, surprises,
hanging out with men in leather jackets and cool sunglasses,
smoking cigarettes and drinking beer at roadside kebab stalls,
racing motorbikes and marking out sacred territories in town,
defending every inch of the land against unwelcome intruders.

    You were also my sister.
You needed me to act as your chaperone
(although I was younger and smaller)
so our parents would allow you out.
You knew you could count on me for everything.
Anything. I was your soldier, your bodyguard,
your companion, your secret admirer. Proud
    as I was, happy as I was,

I knew nothing about your failing grades.
I wasn't aware the headteacher asked Dad
to take you out from the school because
of the fight you'd got into. I had no idea
the family had already decided to send
me to university, not you, because you were
a girl, I was a boy, and we were poor.

They say girls are like wastewater
ready to be poured outdoors when they marry.
They say boys have great futures and must
carry on the family name and make it shine.
They wanted to marry you into a rich family
so you would be better off; so our family
would be better off.

One night you ran away from home,
in tears, after fierce arguments
with Mum, after a slap in the face
from Dad. Mum called you
a black sheep. Dad shouted
never come back. You left home alone.
(I didn't chaperone you this time.)

You moved in with a man
fifteen years your senior, as thin
and tall as a bamboo pole, separated
from his wife but still officially married,
and father to your unborn child.

But you came back, after giving
birth to a baby girl, after bruises
were found on your body. I couldn't
imagine how hard his hands and belt
must have fallen on your slim form,
on your tender skin. Anger ran wild
in the darkness, like roaring floods
overflowing the riverbanks. Apologies
reiterated in the mornings, like eternally
turning prayer wheels. Your tears ran
dry. Your heart was covered with layers
of hard skin.

On a cold winter morning, you stood
outside at the family doorstep, with your
baby daughter, like two frightened birds
shivering after a heavy thunderstorm.

Not a word was spoken about the past.

There was no spring in this northern town.
When winter gave way to summer, you started
to attend evening schools for a college course,
you continued looking after the whole family.

Several years went by.
You got a job at a local college.
Smiles resurfaced on your face.
You gave private tutorials to gain extra income.
You passed the driving test and bought a second-hand car.
You got a mortgage, paid a deposit and moved into a new flat.
You asked Mum and Dad to move in
with you so you could look after them.

Everyone in the neighbourhood spoke highly of you,
praising your beauty, your virtue, your accomplishments,
saying daughters could also be useful
(except they still can't carry on family names,
unlike the hopeless son who chose to stay away
from home and live in another city, neglecting
filial duties, hanging out with other men, tarnishing
the family name. The *real* black sheep.) They were the same
people who had once spoken of you in contempt, calling
you a scandal, a whore, a worn-out shoe nobody wants.

You drove your daughter to university and told her
to be strong and confident. You continued to live
with Mum and Dad, taking care of them in their old
age, without complaints. Suitors and matchmakers
appeared at your doorstep, like bees, like ants, carrying
sweet words with them.

I only saw you occasionally, when I made short,
infrequent visits to a town I no longer called home.

That day you drove me to the airport,
I was sitting next to you, examining your grey hair
glittering in the afternoon sun, carrying
the fragrance of summer. I was happy,
as happy as a child, as if I was still a child,
   sitting on the back of your motorbike,
   holding you tight, holding tight my hero,
   holding tight my life, love, protector, saviour.

I asked if you would consider
remarrying. You didn't reply.
   I needed ask no further.

   I told you my current research
was on feminism. I was hoping, and half expecting,
you'd ask me why. Except you didn't.

   As the car drove quietly and steadily,
   throwing the hometown behind us,
   throwing our childhood behind us,

I would have said:
   Sister, do you know,
everything about feminism I learned
from you, for you, and because of you?

Suitcase

How many things could you stuff
        into a suitcase? I'd no idea.
Layers of clothes, from summer to winter,
packets of snacks padding every corner,
        and yet you knew no end:
One more thing, you'll need this!

        You knelt on the suitcase,
pressing it down and zipping it up,
using the full weight and length
of your body. I felt embarrassed
by your clumsiness. I lost patience
with your nagging. *Stop it, enough!*

You wheeled the suitcase out
onto the pavement and hailed
a cab. You tried to lift it up but failed.
I took over: *Let me do it, Mum.*
        You are too old for this!

I climbed into the cab and waved.
Go home now! It's cold outside!
You stood still, silently watching
the taxi pulling out of your sight.

I waved again, till you became
a small, black dot, pasted on the rear
window. So far. And yet so close.

The suitcase went through on a conveyor
        belt into a dark and cold cabin.
After a hundred years of yearning,
after a thousand years of solitude,
        it came out, awaiting
        an unknown destiny.

I lifted the rock-heavy suitcase
    off the rolling belt, dragging it
    towards my uncertain future.
The red tag you tethered to the handle was
    waving like a hand, your hand;
    beating like a heart, your heart,
    across miles and years.

Diaspora

Diaspora (daɪ ˈæspərə) [a. Gr. διασπορά dispersion, f. διασπείρ-ειν to disperse, f. διά through + σπείρειν to sow, scatter.] (Oxford English Dictionary)

I think of life as a sunflower
that reaches high into the sky.
Dewdrops on fresh petals
glisten in silver moonlight
and sparkle in golden sunshine.

Or a dandelion clock,
unrooted as it draws a full circle,
torn apart by an untimely wind,
carried towards a strange land
for an unknown destiny.

Or New Year fireworks
that shoot from the darkest corners of the earth
into the highest night sky
warming up the frozen faces
of happy families
and lonely travellers.

Misunderstanding

I hope you weren't
too surprised when I said
I was lonely and felt
homesick when you asked
me *how are you?*

I also thought
it was a good idea
when you suggested
*we must meet up again
soon!*

Then you shouldn't
really have needed
my constant reminder
of our appointment;
after three days,
and then a week.

So we met up
at your place
for a drink.
That drink happened to be
whiskey and beer.
Not tea or coffee.
But that was OK
for I was thirsty.

You asked me to make
myself *at home*. So I did.
Perhaps that explained
why I missed the last
train home and had to
stay over.

I ended up sleeping
in the same bed
with you because your sofa
was too small
and it looked
very uncomfortable.

That turned out
to be a nice
misunderstanding.

On a Northern Train

We stood
    next to each other,
        your face glistening with sweat,
            your eyes half-closed in boredom.
            Ed Sheeran was humming
                  in your ears over the headphones.

            Suddenly, the train came
            to a grinding halt.
          Your feet stumbled,
        your body leaned,
      as you collapsed
onto me.

I could smell your body odour.
I could sense the softness hidden
    underneath your rough skin.
I could feel the weight and warmth
    of your body.

Sorry mate, you apologised
in a heavy Northern accent,
while you were trying
    to stand up
    straight
    and hold on
    to the luggage rack.

No worries. I smiled back
while I was trying to conceal
    my disappointment.

                You took out the phone. Your eyes
              were glinting, clandestinely, oscillating
            between the shimmering screen, the fast-
        disappearing sceneries outside
    the window
and me.

Waltzing on the Pavement

The music stopped.
    Your eyes caught mine.
    My eyes caught yours.
I could feel my heart pumping.
    You held out a hand:
Shall we go outside?

I nodded and followed you.
The cold air made me shiver.
    I could feel my sweat.
You pulled me over and gave me
a gentle hug. Your chest was warm.
    Your face was prickly.

Some men in police uniforms walked
our way. Unconsciously, my hands twitched,
my feet fidgeted. You grabbed my hands,
both of them, and held them tightly.
    I could hear your heartbeat.
    You could feel my heartbeat.

The men walked past. A few random looks
but nothing more. The sky didn't fall in.
The earth didn't crack open. We looked
    each other in the eye and smiled.

    The air was still chilly.
    The traffic still noisy.
    Our arms were raised,
    Our hands were linked
as if we were dancing the waltz
nude, on a warm, sunny beach.

In the Printer Room

This guy is quite handsome. I've never seen him here before. He looks fit and his cologne smells nice. When I walk past, he smiles. When he smiles, he shows clean, white teeth. He must be a frequent visitor to the dentist or a religious follower of the dentist's instructions: brush your teeth after you get up, brush your teeth after you have breakfast, brush your teeth after coffee, take no sugar with your coffee and no milk with your tea. What fun is there in life if you have to follow all these rules? How many times must you brush your teeth every morning? The morning time is tight, how do you find time to brush your teeth again and again? I'm a night owl. I go to bed late and get up late and hardly have any time for breakfast. I run to the bus stop to catch the 34 which is always about to pull away. The 34 is the indigo bus, not the 36 which is navy blue. They both start at the Market Square and their stops are next to each other. But the 34 takes you to work, and the 36 takes you to Chilwell Road, where the houses are identical and grey. But at least some of the occupiers own these places. I'm renting a small flat in the city centre, paying rent and utility bills every month. The estate agent says they'll raise next year's rent because of rising costs. My bills are also going up. It's not near the end of the month yet and I'm already on credit. I've used my credit card for shops, bars and buses. These days you don't have to top up a Robin Hood card, you can simply swipe your credit card, and everything's done. Easy. I still have a Robin Hood card in my drawer somewhere, with some credit on it, about five quid I think. I hope they don't take the credit away from me. I'll use it one day, or perhaps give it to someone new to the city, such as my friend Peter who is coming to visit me this weekend. Peter is a wonderful guy and he looks very attractive, or shall I say I'm attracted to him? We met at a club on Canal Street in Manchester. He smiled at me. I smiled at him too. He then took my hand and dragged me onto the dance floor. The music and alcohol made me happy. He made me happy. He's a cheerful person and always has plenty of energy for fun. When he smiles, he shows his clean, white teeth, like this guy who's standing next to me in front of the printer. This guy. Peter.

In Front of the Left Lion

No introduction
was needed.
My foreign face
is the name tag I carry
in this strange city.
I waved back and grinned
as you walked up.

That day you wore
a blue T-shirt, I wore
a red T-shirt. We could be
representing the two sides
of British politics.
I stood still, not knowing
what to do. Elbow greeting
felt new to me.

You asked me
where I came from.
You asked about
my life as an international
student. You suggested
we go for a drink.

There we were, sitting
by the window inside
Lord Roberts, watching
the world go by.
The afternoon sun
coloured the window,
the beer glass,
and my mood.

You were enthusiastic
and talkative. I was shy,
struggling to express myself
in a foreign language.

Your face lit up, as you
reminisced about your last trip
to Asia. You attempted
a few Japanese words
which I didn't understand

but that made me laugh.
Your eagerness to please me
and your childlike innocence
was infectious. Perhaps
I'd already been charmed
by you, a guy I'd only
recently met online.

You asked me
about my hometown.
A feeling of sadness
dawned on me.

My hometown was still
in lockdown. My parents
still had to do daily tests.
My last home visit was
three years ago,

before everyone talked
about the 'China virus',
before I was spat on
and shouted at by strangers,
before I learned what
being a foreigner might mean
in a post-Brexit land.
On those lonely winter nights,
I missed home,
and food,
and language,
and an intimate touch.

Gently
you put your hand
on my shoulder
and hugged me.
Your hands were
big, and your arms
were strong.

You said your nan
passed away last year
alone and lonely
in the middle
of the lockdown.
You said you missed her
and her cooking.
You said you had many
sleepless nights.

That moment
we were hugging
each other in a small pub.
Time froze.
The crowd vanished.
The world mattered
no more.

Soon we would part
and become strangers
in life. But that didn't
matter. A warm hug
on a cold winter afternoon
was all I needed
to feel at home.

It was also
what you needed
to connect
to a man
and his culture.

Leather Man

You stood
in the crowded bar.
Your padded leather jacket.
Your broad shoulders.
Your pumped muscles.
Your weathered face.
Your stubble beard.
Your aloofness seemed so out
of place here, in a place full
of fabulous queers
and fierce drag queens.

Our eyes met across
the colour-lit dancefloor.
You stared at me;
at my skimpy T-shirt and skinny jeans,
my pink lips and purple eyelashes.

Relax, leather man.
Take off your mask,
put away your pretentiousness.
Let's sashay
in the style of RuPaul
to the music of Lady Gaga
till we shed away
all the weight that burdens
you, and me.

While I was looking
at you, you were looking
at me, almost as fascinated
as I was with you. When our eyes
met, a ripple spread
across the smooth dance floor.
Who had thrown the first look?

Skin

That day you sat on a Harley-Davidson in full leather,
your muscles bulged in the skin's tight grip.

Leather is, after all, a type of skin.
A love for leather is also a love for skin.

Wearing a chest harness underneath my jacket,
I could feel its pull, its restraint, and my pounding heart.

I straddled the bike and held you tight, breathing
your body and feeling its temperature, texture, mesmerised

by the imagination of its pre- and current life
as I was drawn to, absorbed by, and becoming part of it.

You are older and I'm younger. I don't care. You are
what they call Caucasian, I'm Asian, all that cliché.

Call it fetish; call it commodity fetish, sexual fetish, racial fetish.
Stop worrying about my identity, your identity, this and that label.

Let me feel the roughness and tenderness of your hands, arms and lips.
Let me dissolve into your skin, your body, your Harley-Davidson.

Ring

In darkness I submit myself
   to your hairy torso
      to your muscular legs
         to your firm hand
            to your rough skin
               to every tender moment
            and movement
         of my hand
      my mouth
my tongue
   to the saltiness and sweetness of you
         to the pulsing and throbbing of my desire.

My lips let out a smile
   as my tongue touches
      and chases
         a ring,
         a small ring,
         a small, metal ring,
         a ring that was once your secret,
            and has now become our secret,
         a ring that is being
      enveloped by my tongue
   tingling between my teeth
and shining in my head.

Morning Tea

Every morning
I wake up to the whistle
of a boiling kettle, like an old
Victorian steam engine, the creak
of wooden floorboards,
a dark shadow hovering
over my bed,

the hot smell
and strong taste
of Yorkshire Tea, filled
with your love, almost
overflowing, gargled
down my throat,
almost gagging.

This isn't a murder
mystery. It is our
morning tea ritual.

The tea isn't the 龍井, 大紅袍
or 鐵觀音 I was used to.
(And my Mum would certainly
frown if she ever saw you
pour milk into the tea.)
But it still tastes like tea,
and it makes me feel at home.

Calling Home

The moment you walked
into my room while I was calling
home was the moment I dreaded
the most. I was speaking
to my family in China via WeChat
in rusty Mandarin.

*Hey Mum hey Dad hey Sister
hey Xiaoyu hey Bailing.
How are you how's everyone
how's the lockdown situation at home?
Have you eaten what have you eaten
what else have you eaten?
No I haven't had dinner yet
because I've just got up.
No I don't need to put on more clothes
because it's summer here.
Yes I'm fine everything's fine
please don't worry about me.
Yes Covid figures are rising but I'm safe
and healthy and staying at home.*

I didn't tell them I recently caught
Covid and still felt weak.
Or about the young guys who shouted
Coronavirus at me on the high street.
Nor my stress at work.
Nor my frustration with British politics.
Nor how and what you were doing.
I didn't mention
your name.

Nor did they ask
about you.
(They may or may not know
I'm gay. They may or may not know
we're married. We simply don't
talk about it.)

I was nervous
while you were standing there
listening (as if you understood
Mandarin), for I was afraid
to show my other self
to you, a strange person
you don't quite understand –

a strange person even I
don't quite understand.

The World's End

That Christmas,
you took me to the village
where you grew up
in North Yorkshire.
A village whose name you said
could be found in the Domesday
Book. A name I couldn't
remember or pronounce,
though I briefly philosophised
about the end of the world.

The village was tucked
deep in endless hills and dales
and moors covered by patches
of snow and ice
and dry heather.
Grey sky.
Low clouds.
Vast land.
Winding road.
Black stone houses.
Perhaps it was indeed
the world's end.

The smell of roast turkey
floated in the air.
Your Mum was busy preparing
the table while your Dad
was sitting on the sofa watching
boring Christmas television.
The noise was hypnotising.
At least it saved us
some small talk.

We took our seats, thanked
whoever had brought us dinner
(anyone but your Mum)

and helped ourselves to boiled
vegetables, roast potatoes, pigs
in blankets.

Lots of things were said
about neighbours and relatives.
Not much was mentioned
about you
and me.

I smiled and nodded,
as if I understood
your heavy accents.
You seemed to have changed
into a different person:
polite, reserved
and straight.

The moment
I enjoyed the most
was the ritual when we grabbed
both ends of the crackers
and pulled them apart.
Bang! Bang! Bang! Bang!
There came
the magic crowns, red and
green and purple and yellow.
We put them
on our heads, proudly
competing for silliness.
We laughed
at one another
in childlike innocence.

You took me to a pub.
A local pub for local people.
A pub where a red and white
St. George's flag flew
high on the roof.

There, men drank dark ale.
Men threw darts.
Men played pool.
Men bantered with mates
about football and women.
(There were no women in the pub.)
Men looked at you, me
and us, in curiosity
and slight hostility.

I must've been
the first Chinese
they'd seen in the pub.
We must've been
the first gay couple
to have patronised
the place. We made
history and brought
juicy gossip to this
quiet village.

Early next morning,
we bade farewell to your tired parents,
to the sheep that grazed on,
to the dog that barked at us,
to the school building you hated so much,
to the church you refused to step back in.
I didn't ask you
what it was like
to grow up
in the village.

Driving along
the zigzagging road
across the hills,
the moors,
the rocks,
the heather,
the patches of snow and ice

and childhood memories,
you threw your home
behind, just as I'd done
to my hometown.
(Although one is in England,
the other in China;
one has a population of five hundred,
the other, seven million.)

Was it this
that had brought us together?

Fireflies

When I think of you, I think of the spontaneous departures we made, throwing our clothes and essentials in two rucksacks, striding on the motorbike, letting the roaring engine and the winding road take us to unexpected destinations. I think of our long rides on the bike, sitting on the back, holding fast, breaking the wind and travelling in time and space. I think of the many stops we made on the way, initially for a short comfort break but often having our breath taken away by sublime mountain ranges or mirror-like lakes. I think of the many cold nights we camped out, holding each other tightly to keep warm, while stars hung high and fireflies hovered in the air. Those were happy times. Your vivid smile. My unbound heart.

Then we would come back to the city, to our small flat. Surrounded by polluted air, ceaseless traffic and noisy, nosy neighbours. Back to the oven, the washer, the vacuum cleaner. Back to never-ending work and constantly rising utility bills. The lively, energetic you disappeared in the concrete jungles, amongst the indifferent faces of the commuters. You smoked heavily. You lost your temper easily. We had fights. Our personality differences were redefined as cultural differences – until one day we decided life couldn't carry on like this. I moved out of your flat. Nights without you were difficult, but I survived.

On starry nights like this, I often wonder if you still ride your bike, if you still travel to our favourite places, if you still think of me when you gaze into the horizon and see the twinkling lights. Like stars. Like fireflies. Like the free spirits we were.

The Key

After all these years,
I still hold on to your key,
although you have moved
to another city, although the flat's
owner or the next tenant may
have changed the lock
many a time.

It's a well-used,
small, bronze key
attached to a silver
heart-shaped ring.
It appears so light,
yet feels so heavy.

I am sorry I forgot
to give back the key
when I left your flat
that morning, when I took
a last look at you, at the room
where we'd spent
so much time
together.

Perhaps
I just wanted
to hold on
to your space,
your body,
your heart,
your memory
for as long
as I could.

Haunted Village

The village is haunted
      by hungry ghosts from the Great Famine,
      unrepenting souls from the Cultural Revolution,
      deserted baby girls from the One-Child Policy.

They were cursed at birth,
      expelled from homes,
      erased from memories.

The village well remains dilapidated,
      its depth measured by stares,
      its moss moistened by tears.

Weeping willows stand desolately by the river,
      the widows' hair entangled with the tree roots.
      their souls drifting amongst the water lilies.

No wind can muffle their voices.
No sand can efface their apparitions.

From death they will rise, unrooting red chastity pillars,
      demolishing Confucian temples and ancestor halls,
      chasing and hanging bloodthirsty patriarchs,
      making this a village of vengeance.

April in Shanghai

'Shanghai's 25 million residents have been shut in their homes for weeks while officials try to contain a severe Covid-19 outbreak ... It's now five weeks since Shanghai's population was first ordered to stay at home as part of an extremely strict lockdown.' (BBC News, 23 April 2022)

They say April is the cruellest
month, when chilly winds from the north
empty the crowded city streets
and shut millions of doors.

Concrete barriers and metal fences
block the hope out of bounds.
The disinfecting odour of despair
permeates every inch of the city's air.

Can you see the helpless looks of those
with homes they can't return to?
Can you hear the devastating cries of those
forcibly taken away from their loved ones?

Shanghai, the heroic city,
your pride is shattered,
your tears run dry.

Birds hover in the sky.
Grass rambles on the pavement.
Dandelions blossom along the barricades.

When thunder roars on the horizon,
when lightning flashes in the night sky,
you know you will be reborn.
Like birds. Like grass. Like dandelions.

White Paper

'Blank sheets of white A4 paper became a symbol. Protesters held them to symbolise the lack of freedom of speech – speaking out without explicitly saying anything.' (BBC News, 7 December 2022)

When anger becomes infectious,
when words are seen to be dangerous,
leave me blank, please!

The day you lift me up
    with your shivering hands
    as if I were
    as heavy as a rock,
    as dazzling as the sun,

I see my peers, my fellows, my comrades,
    standing together,
        in the wind,
            like leaves,
                like sea waves, spreading
                      into the future.

Light me, and let the fire rage!
At least this will give the world
a glimmer of light, warmth and hope.

Liverpool, 1946

An erasure poem based on MP Kim Johnson's Speech in the UK Parliament, 21 July 2021, on 'Forced Repatriation of Chinese Seamen from Liverpool After World War Two'.

20,000
Chinese seamen worked
in the shipping industry.
Thousands
gave their lives under bombardment.
About 2,000
survived, returned to Liverpool.

Behind closed doors,
in corridors of power,
decisions to remove
set in motion.

Expel 'undesirables'!
Home Office
amend papers.

October 1945,
secret meeting
in Whitehall.
Opening of a new file –
contents
not to be discussed.

The following July,
Liverpool constabulary
carried out orders
to round up
and forcibly repatriate.

Immigration wagons
prowling the streets.
Seizing men.
Forcing into houses.
Undercover officers.
Seize documents.
Erase records.

About 2,000 deported.
Snatched from homes.
Dumped on shores
left decades before.

Wives and partners
abandoned with children.
Suffering trauma.

Decades later,
declassified records
reveal
untold grief.

Oriental Pavilion

While we are starving
for food, in the cold wind,
the red lantern above the door
catches our eyes.

Let's have a chinky! my white
British friend shouts.
(I frown, not sure if I should
tell him off.)
Bad translation! my Chinese
friend exclaims.
(An English sign reads
'Oriental Pavilion'
above the Chinese name
'the moon reflected on the water pond'.)

Our feeble legs
can hold no longer.
Our empty stomachs
allow no intellectual debate.

Greeting us is a beckoning cat
that never tires of waving
and the beaming
face of the waitress
(who's also the usher, the cashier,
the manager, the restaurant owner).
She takes our order and hands it
over to the kitchen. (Perhaps
to her husband who's also
the chef.) In no time we can hear
the wok sizzling.

What aroma, what a sight, what delight!
There's our favourite
Kung Pao chicken, with red chillies
decorating honey-glazed meat.
There are also Mapo tofu, sweet
and sour pork, served with
steamed rice and hot
jasmine tea, enticing
our appetites. The sun
is bright, and life
is good again.

We strike up a conversation
with the woman. Her family
has lived here for over
a decade. At the beginning, life
was hard, until the restaurant
won the hearts (or stomachs) of the locals.

Life in the small town was mostly
quiet. Sometimes drunks stayed late, refused
to leave, shop windows were smashed.
Last year, graffiti appeared on the door:
China virus (although the family was
not from China), *Go back to
your own country!* (though there's
no place for them to go back to).

Now the pandemic
is over, business is back
to normal, although bills
are rising and inflation
is high. She's sent her son
to school and then college, hoping
he'll be able to deal
with the tax office,
the police, the local gangs.

She's talking about her life
as a migrant, and the prejudice
she's experienced. She can't
put a name to it.

Shall I tell her it's racism
and xenophobia she's experienced?
Shall I tell her the restaurant name
is a bad translation?
Shall I let my white, British
friend know the word 'chinky'
is deeply offensive?

We look at the woman
with humility and respect.
But we, all of us,
can only say
the food was delicious!
and nod as we walk
away.

A Trip to the Peak District

A rundown pub tucked in a sleepy village.
A warm Sunday roast served on a chilly day.
A pint gargled down the throat. I'm becoming
      more English with every drop of ale I drink.

A few odd looks are thrown this way.
You frown at me. For you I'm a stranger,
outsider, student, tourist, foreigner, migrant;
      undeserving of a smile, or kindness.

Chink, you clench your teeth and fist.
      Go back to your own country!
My country? I repeat to myself. I've got no country.
      A queer migrant has no country.

But there's no time to ponder. Grabbing
      my bag, I run, as fast as I can.
The rambling country road
      leads nowhere near home.

Eurovision

In the ocean
of colours, the cacophony
of sounds, I see
you – what you imagine
yourself to be: a happy
family of nations, till
the final votes, in a welcoming
place (except for migrants
and refugees), on a peaceful
continent (where wars
are raging on).

I can't see
myself. There's no
East Asian face
on stage,
and in the crowd.

*Asians will never
become Europeans*, they say,
*because they are different
people.* (Are we really
that different?)

Chinese television has banned
Eurovision, for the tattoos,
piercings, rainbow flags,
'Western values and lifestyles'
you represent.

But l still love you.
I love sharing your wild
joys, your cheesy
tunes, your cheap
tears, your glittering
faces, your outlandish
clothing, your magical
douze points
that raises
all my hope
and then breaks
all my heart.

Eurostar

Like a bullet, the train
cuts through white, chilly fog;
through the green fields, saturated
with romanticised war memories,
beneath a stretch of water, *la Manche*,
the sleeve, used to extend greetings,
wave farewells, wipe tears.

On board, the aromas
of coffee, cheese and croissants,
the sound of multilingual
announcements and conversations.
On board, one embodies the being
of a cosmopolitan 'world citizen'.
If Europe is a cosmos, this train
is a bright star. Its glamour hasn't
dwindled after Brexit.

Separating the rail and the land,
on both sides, stand tall fences.
Fences made of iron and steel and razor wire,
overseen by security guards
and countless cameras. Fences
reminding me of the Berlin Wall.
Fences separating life from death, hope
from despair, this world from that world.

For some, a couple of hours feels like an eternity.

The train plunges deep into the dark.
Apparitions superimpose on mirror-like
windows. Smiling faces. Crying faces.
Faces of horror. Faces of empathy, only
illuminated by flickering lights that fly past.

In my mind's eye,
swarms of fish roam freely around us.

Christmas in Beeston

Rows of red terrace houses, soaked wet against a grey sky.
Orange lights glitter on the pavement as the night's curtain falls.

Which house owns what car is for all to see.
Whether a family is happy or sad one only has to listen.

The old lady, next door to the left, is quiet as a hermit.
She's gained more visitors since the death of her chain-smoking husband.

The Chinese girls, next door to the right, study very hard.
People say they are the best tenants as they don't party loud.

The young guy opposite games late into the night,
undisturbed by the baby whose scream pierces the sky.

The pizzeria on the street corner is as busy as ever.
The English owner has painted on its wall a Leaning Tower of Pisa.

The Greek café has tables outside even though it's wet and cold.
Just a few doors down, the smell of Turkish kebab lingers in the air.

A halal grocer sits next door to a Chinese restaurant.
A local pub has Sky Sports on its window against a Union Jack.

Charity shops and estate agents compete for attention.
As a local shop closes down, a chain store opens.

When Christmas lights and New Year fireworks illuminate the sky,
everything and nothing will be the same for another blasted year.

Lunar New Year

When fireworks light up the sky, announcing
the beginning of the Lunar New Year
(*some call it Chinese New Year or
the Spring Festival, but I praise the moon*),
when loud firecrackers and red spring couplets
join hands to expel evil spirits (*along with all
the nightmares from the pandemic lockdown*),
when families are gathering for dumplings
or glutenous rice cakes (*Are you sure they're
happy? What about those who live alone
or who don't do this?*) I'm thinking of you.

I'm thinking of the millions who lost their lives
or their loved ones during the pandemic
(*and the millions more who lost their work,
home or hope*). I'm thinking of the funerals
that took place at the same time as the New Year
celebrations. (*Should this be a season of joy
or mourning?*) I'm thinking of the people who were
jailed because they raised a piece of white paper.
(*The paper remained silent, even when
burnt, thrown away, or torn apart.*)

I'm thinking of the physical or verbal abuse
Asians receive because of how they look.
(*'You're Chinese, you deserve it!'*)
I'm thinking of the Asian women shot dead
in Atlanta because of a white man's obsession
(*and the community who were denied rights
to mourning*). I'm thinking of the gunshots
that shattered the glass of the dance studio
in Monterey Park, California. (*Why so much hatred?*)

The Year of the Tiger was fierce, but it's finally gone. (*Perhaps no valorisation of meat-eating creatures in the future.*) The Year of the Rabbit arrives quietly and discreetly (*and may more people become vegetarian or vegan this year*). I'm thinking of you, me, and us, still separated by the oceans. And I'm thinking of the day when we'll finally meet, sometime, somewhere.

Snow in March

It's snowing in March.
Feather-like flakes are dancing
in the air. You are complaining
about the cold, the wet, the nuisance.
I am thinking about how lightly
and infrequently it snows
on this island kissed
by jet streams and threatened
by global warming.

That I saw much heavier
snow in my childhood
in a small Inner Mongolian
town where the Siberian High
was a permanent resident,
where the thick, white blanket
covered the ground for almost
half a year, where children charged
forward on sleighs, leaving
smooth, parallel trails in the snow,
where adults chiselled the ice
open and nets and nets of fish
arose from the frozen lakes.

That I left my hometown to study
in Beijing, where in spring strong
winds threw bitter sands onto the face,
except when it was snowing, when the air
was clean and crisp, when the Weiming Lake
was sheltered in snow, surrounded silently
by white pine trees, silver cypresses.

That I lay on a bright
sandy beach in Sydney, surrounded
by nude bodies and pure Aussie
happiness, where the blueness
of the sea merged with the azure

of the sky in the dazzlingly
white sunlight. I wondered
what it would be like to lie
on the snow.

That I walked in the snow
for a couple of miles, making
my way through a small forest
in a Berlin suburb, to an old
building where I would meet
other migrants, refugees,
Europe's 'others', trying
to figure out the difference
between accusatives and datives,
trying to build a new life
in a cold climate.

That I arrived in London
on a snowy day and managed
to settle down after all
the phone calls, long queues,
missed paperwork, repeated
apologies. You helped me
remove my suitcase from the car
boot and opened the front door
guarded by colourful garden
gnomes smiling in the snow.

That I still miss the sun
and the beach. That often,
in my dreams, emerge
the small Mongolian town,
parallel trails chasing the sleighs;
the frozen Weiming Lake,
silver contours of the cypresses;
the small forest in Berlin,
zigzagging footprints stretching on;
the multi-coloured garden gnomes
smiling in the snow.

Here in the Midlands
there's no extreme
weather, no intense
love or hate. Quietly
we grow old, just like
the silent

f
a
l
l

of the
snowflakes

dancing
in the air

and melting
before they
land.

Acknowledgments

Earlier versions of some poems ('April in Shanghai', 'A Trip to the Peak District', 'But Where Do You Really Come From?', 'Calling Home', 'Christmas in Beeston', 'Confession of the Rabbit God', 'Diaspora', 'Fireflies', 'In Front of the Left Lion', 'Morning Tea', 'Misunderstanding', 'Qu Yuan', 'Suitcase', 'Snow', 'The Magic Pot', 'The World's End', 'Wildest Dreams') first appeared in 詩集: *An Anthology* (edited by Will Harris), *Contemporary Theatre Review*, *Maria Lazar: Poetry from Exile* (edited by Kathleen Dunmore), *Messy Misfits Club*, *Migrant Diaries*, *The Rialto*, *Positions Politics*, *the other side of hope*, *The Voice & Verse Poetry Magazine* and *Write On*. I thank all the editors of these publications for their encouragements and valuable feedback. I am grateful to the Valley Press editor Jamie McGarry for believing in the value of this book and for his insightful editorial suggestions.

I would like to thank Joanna Barnard, Natalie Linh Bolderston, Brad Gyori, Will Harris, Maria Jastrzębska, Gayathiri Kamalakanthan, Ali Lewis, Glyn Maxwell, Leanne Moden, Shivanee Ramlochan, Anna Robinson, Sarah Wardle and Tom White, whose poetry workshops have been inspiring. Thanks also go to fellow poets and writers who attended these workshops for their peer support. In Nottingham, I have been fortunate to find myself in the middle of a vibrant poetry scene and in the company of wonderful people from several poetry groups including Dandelions Poetry, DIY Poets, Fluent in Both, GOBS Collective, Open Book, Paper Crane Poetry, Notts Poetry and World Jam. Kudos to the fantastic reading community clustering around Five Leaves Bookshop. Thanks also go to Phil Cowley and Sam Ruddock for offering constructive comments on earlier versions of my work.

I am indebted to my family in China and the UK for their unconditional love, and all my queer and Asian friends for their support – they are the reasons for this book's existence.